Easy Cooking Recipes Without Onions

Welcome to "Easy Cooking Recipes Without Onions"! This cookbook is dedicated to those who want to enjoy delicious and aromatic dishes without the use of onions. Whether you have dietary restrictions, allergies, or simply prefer onion-free meals, this collection of recipes will satisfy your cravings and tantalize your taste buds.

Table of Contents:

Soups and Starters
1.1. Creamy Potato Leek Soup
1.2. Tomato Basil Bisque
1.3. Butternut Squash Soup
1.4. Garlic and Herb Hummus
1.5. Spinach and Artichoke Dip

Salads and Dressings
2.1. Caprese Salad
2.2. Greek Salad
2.3. Avocado Cilantro Lime Dressing
2.4. Creamy Dijon Vinaigrette
2.5. Mango and Basil Salad

Main Dishes
3.1. Lemon Herb Roast Chicken
3.2. Beef Stroganoff
3.3. Grilled Herb-Marinated Salmon
3.4. Mushroom and Spinach Stuffed Bell Peppers
3.5. Eggplant Parmesan

Pasta and Rice
4.1. Creamy Pesto Pasta
4.2. Mushroom Risotto
4.3. Spinach and Ricotta Stuffed Shells
4.4. Lemon Garlic Shrimp Linguine
4.5. Thai Peanut Noodles

Sides and Accompaniments
5.1. Roasted Garlic Mashed Potatoes
5.2. Lemon Herb Quinoa
5.3. Honey Glazed Carrots
5.4. Grilled Asparagus with Balsamic Glaze
5.5. Cucumber and Mint Raita

Breads and Baking
6.1. Rosemary Focaccia
6.2. Cheddar and Chive Biscuits
6.3. Herbed Dinner Rolls
6.4. Zucchini and Parmesan Muffins
6.5. Chocolate Chip Banana Bread

Desserts
7.1. Mixed Berry Crisp
7.2. Vanilla Custard
7.3. Apple Cinnamon Galette
7.4. Chocolate Avocado Mousse
7.5. Coconut Rice Pudding

1.1. Creamy Potato Leek Soup (Onion-Free)

Servings: 4-6

Ingredients:

- 3 large leeks, white and light green parts only, thoroughly cleaned and sliced
- 3 tablespoons unsalted butter
- 4 large russet potatoes, peeled and diced
- 4 cups vegetable broth
- 1 cup heavy cream
- 2 cloves garlic, minced
- 2 teaspoons fresh thyme leaves, plus more for garnish
- Salt and pepper, to taste
- Chopped chives, for garnish (optional)

Instructions:

1- In a large pot, melt the butter over medium heat. Add the sliced leeks and sauté for about 5-7 minutes, until they are soft and slightly translucent. Stir occasionally to prevent browning.

2- Add the minced garlic to the leeks and cook for an additional 1-2 minutes until fragrant.

3- Add the diced potatoes to the pot, along with the fresh thyme leaves. Stir to combine and coat the potatoes with the buttery leek mixture.

4- Pour in the vegetable broth, ensuring that the potatoes are submerged. Increase the heat to medium-high and bring the mixture to a boil. Once boiling, reduce the heat to low, cover the pot, and let the soup simmer for about 20-25 minutes, or until the potatoes are tender and easily pierced with a fork.

5- Using an immersion blender or regular blender (in batches if necessary), carefully blend the soup until smooth and creamy. If using a regular blender, return the blended soup to the pot.

6- Slowly pour in the heavy cream while stirring to combine. Allow the soup to heat through over low heat, but do not let it come to a boil.

7- Taste the soup and season with salt and pepper to your preference. Remember that the vegetable broth might already contain some salt.

8- Once the soup is heated and seasoned, ladle it into bowls. Garnish with additional fresh thyme leaves and chopped chives, if desired.

9- Serve the creamy potato leek soup hot, alongside crusty bread or your favorite side dish.

Note: Leeks have a mild onion-like flavor. If you're looking to completely avoid any onion flavor, you can omit the leeks and replace them with an equivalent amount of chopped celery for a slightly different but still delicious variation of the soup.

1.2. Tomato Basil Bisque (Onion-Free)

Servings: 4-6

Ingredients:

- 2 tablespoons unsalted butter
- 2 carrots, peeled and diced
- 2 celery stalks, diced
- 2 cloves garlic, minced
- 2 (28-ounce) cans whole peeled tomatoes
- 1 teaspoon dried basil
- 1/2 teaspoon dried oregano
- 1/2 teaspoon dried thyme
- 2 cups vegetable broth
- 1 cup heavy cream
- Salt and pepper, to taste
- Fresh basil leaves, for garnish
- Grated Parmesan cheese, for garnish (optional)

Instructions:

1- In a large pot, melt the butter over medium heat. Add the diced carrots and celery. Sauté for about 5-7 minutes, until the vegetables start to soften.
2- Add the minced garlic to the pot and cook for an additional 1-2 minutes until fragrant.
3- Drain the canned tomatoes and roughly chop them. Add the chopped tomatoes, dried basil, dried oregano, and dried thyme to the pot. Stir well to combine with the sautéed vegetables.
4- Pour in the vegetable broth and bring the mixture to a simmer. Allow it to cook for about 15-20 minutes, stirring occasionally, to let the flavors meld.

5- Using an immersion blender or regular blender (in batches if necessary), carefully blend the soup until smooth and creamy. If using a regular blender, return the blended soup to the pot.

6- Slowly pour in the heavy cream while stirring to combine. Heat the soup over low heat, making sure it doesn't come to a boil.

7- Taste the bisque and season with salt and pepper according to your taste. Once heated through and seasoned, ladle the tomato basil bisque into bowls.

8- Garnish each serving with fresh basil leaves and a sprinkle of grated Parmesan cheese, if desired.

9- Serve the tomato basil bisque hot, accompanied by crusty bread or your favorite side.

Note: This tomato basil bisque recipe offers a delightful blend of flavors without the use of onions. The carrots and celery add natural sweetness and depth to the soup. Feel free to adjust the seasoning and consistency according to your preference.

1.3. Creamy Butternut Squash Soup (Onion-Free)

Servings: 4-6

Ingredients:

- 1 medium butternut squash, peeled, seeded, and cubed
- 2 carrots, peeled and chopped
- 2 celery stalks, chopped
- 2 cloves garlic, minced
- 3 tablespoons unsalted butter
- 4 cups vegetable broth
- 1 teaspoon dried thyme
- 1/2 teaspoon ground cinnamon
- 1/4 teaspoon ground nutmeg
- Salt and pepper, to taste
- 1 cup heavy cream
- Chopped fresh parsley or chives, for garnish

Instructions:

1- In a large pot, melt the butter over medium heat. Add the chopped carrots and celery. Sauté for about 5-7 minutes, until the vegetables begin to soften.

2- Add the minced garlic to the pot and cook for an additional 1-2 minutes until fragrant.

3- Add the cubed butternut squash to the pot, along with the dried thyme, ground cinnamon, and ground nutmeg. Stir to combine and coat the vegetables with the butter and spices.

4- Pour in the vegetable broth, ensuring that the squash is submerged. Increase the heat to medium-high and bring the mixture to a boil. Once boiling, reduce the heat to low, cover the pot, and let the soup simmer for about 20-25 minutes, or until the butternut squash is tender and easily pierced with a fork.

5- Using an immersion blender or regular blender (in batches if necessary), carefully blend the soup until smooth and creamy. If using a regular blender, return the blended soup to the pot.

6- Slowly pour in the heavy cream while stirring to combine. Heat the soup over low heat, but do not let it come to a boil.

7- Taste the soup and season with salt and pepper to your preference.

8- Once the soup is heated through and seasoned, ladle it into bowls.

9- Garnish each serving with chopped fresh parsley or chives for a burst of color and freshness.

10- Serve the creamy butternut squash soup hot, accompanied by crusty bread or a side salad.

Note: This onion-free butternut squash soup is a perfect blend of creamy and comforting flavors. The combination of butternut squash, carrots, and celery provides a delightful sweetness and depth to the soup. Adjust the seasonings and consistency to suit your taste. Enjoy the heartwarming flavors of this soup as a starter or a light meal.

1.4. Garlic and Herb Hummus (Onion-Free)

Servings: 6-8

Ingredients:

- 2 (15-ounce) cans chickpeas, drained and rinsed
- 3 cloves garlic, minced
- 1/4 cup tahini
- 1/4 cup fresh lemon juice
- 1/4 cup extra-virgin olive oil
- 1 teaspoon ground cumin

- 1/2 teaspoon paprika
- 1/4 teaspoon cayenne pepper (adjust to taste)
- 1 teaspoon dried oregano
- 1 teaspoon dried thyme
- Salt and pepper, to taste
- Chopped fresh parsley, for garnish
- Drizzle of olive oil, for serving

Instructions:

1- In a food processor, combine the chickpeas, minced garlic, tahini, lemon juice, and extra-virgin olive oil. Process until smooth and creamy, scraping down the sides as needed.

2- Add the ground cumin, paprika, cayenne pepper, dried oregano, and dried thyme to the mixture. Blend again until the herbs and spices are fully incorporated.

3- Taste the hummus and season with salt and pepper according to your preference. Adjust the cayenne pepper if you prefer a milder or spicier flavor.

4- If the hummus is too thick, you can add a little water or more olive oil to reach your desired consistency. Blend again until well combined.

5- Transfer the hummus to a serving bowl. Create a well in the center with the back of a spoon.

6- Drizzle a little olive oil over the top of the hummus. Garnish with chopped fresh parsley for a burst of color and a touch of freshness.

7- Serve the garlic and herb hummus with your favorite dippers, such as pita bread, carrot sticks, cucumber slices, or whole-grain crackers.

8- Store any leftover hummus in an airtight container in the refrigerator for up to 5 days.

Note: This onion-free garlic and herb hummus is a delightful and flavorful dip that's perfect for parties, gatherings, or simply as a tasty snack. The combination of fresh garlic and fragrant herbs creates a harmonious balance of flavors. Adjust the seasonings and olive oil to achieve your preferred taste and consistency. Enjoy the creamy goodness of this hummus with a variety of dippers or use it as a spread for sandwiches and wraps.

1.5. Creamy Spinach and Artichoke Dip (Onion-Free)

Servings: 6-8

Ingredients:

- 1 (10-ounce) package frozen chopped spinach, thawed and drained
- 1 (14-ounce) can artichoke hearts, drained and chopped
- 2 cloves garlic, minced
- 1/4 cup mayonnaise
- 1/4 cup sour cream
- 1/2 cup grated Parmesan cheese
- 1 cup shredded mozzarella cheese
- 1/2 teaspoon dried oregano
- 1/2 teaspoon dried thyme
- 1/4 teaspoon red pepper flakes (adjust to taste)
- Salt and pepper, to taste
- Olive oil, for greasing
- Tortilla chips, pita wedges, or sliced vegetables, for dipping

Instructions:

1- Preheat your oven to 375°F (190°C). Grease a baking dish with olive oil, ensuring the bottom and sides are well coated.

2- In a mixing bowl, combine the chopped spinach, chopped artichoke hearts, minced garlic, mayonnaise, sour cream, grated Parmesan cheese, shredded mozzarella cheese, dried oregano, dried thyme, and red pepper flakes. Mix well to evenly distribute all the ingredients.

3- Season the mixture with salt and pepper to your taste. Keep in mind that the cheeses may already contain some salt.

4- Transfer the mixture to the greased baking dish and spread it out evenly.

5- Bake the dip in the preheated oven for about 20-25 minutes, or until the edges are golden and bubbly.

6- Once the dip is cooked, remove it from the oven and let it cool slightly before serving.

7- Serve the creamy spinach and artichoke dip with your choice of dippers, such as tortilla chips, pita wedges, or sliced vegetables.

8- Enjoy the dip while it's warm and gooey, savoring the delightful blend of spinach, artichoke, and cheesy goodness.

9- Leftovers can be stored in an airtight container in the refrigerator for up to 3 days. Reheat in the microwave or oven before serving.

Note: This onion-free spinach and artichoke dip is a crowd-pleasing appetizer that's perfect for parties, game nights, or casual gatherings. The combination of creamy cheeses, spinach, and artichoke hearts creates a delectable and satisfying dip. Adjust the seasonings and red pepper flakes to suit your taste preferences. Serve it alongside your favorite dippers for a delightful snacking experience.

2.1. Caprese Salad (Onion-Free)

Servings: 4

Ingredients:

- 4 large ripe tomatoes, sliced
- 8 ounces fresh mozzarella cheese, sliced
- Fresh basil leaves
- Extra-virgin olive oil
- Balsamic glaze
- Salt and freshly ground black pepper, to taste

Instructions:

1- Wash and slice the tomatoes into rounds of approximately 1/4-inch thickness.
2- Arrange them on a serving platter or individual plates, slightly overlapping. Slice the fresh mozzarella cheese into rounds similar in thickness to the tomato slices.
3- Place a slice of mozzarella on top of each tomato slice.
4- Pick fresh basil leaves and arrange them on top of the mozzarella slices. You can use whole leaves or tear larger leaves into smaller pieces for even distribution.
5- Drizzle extra-virgin olive oil over the tomato, mozzarella, and basil. Use a light hand, as you want to enhance the flavors without overwhelming the dish.
6- Drizzle balsamic glaze over the salad. The amount can vary based on your preference, but a gentle drizzle is generally sufficient.
7- Season the salad with a pinch of salt and a grind of freshly ground black pepper.
8- Serve the caprese salad immediately as a refreshing and visually appealing appetizer or side dish.

Note: This onion-free caprese salad beautifully showcases the harmonious combination of fresh tomatoes, creamy mozzarella, and fragrant basil. The absence of onions allows these key ingredients to shine and create a light and flavorful dish. Adjust the quantities of olive oil, balsamic glaze, and seasonings to your liking. Enjoy the simplicity and elegance of this classic Italian salad.

2.2. Greek Salad (Onion-Free)

Servings: 4

Ingredients:

For the Salad:

- 2 large tomatoes, diced
- 1 cucumber, diced
- 1 green bell pepper, diced
- 1 cup Kalamata olives, pitted
- 1 cup crumbled feta cheese
- 1/2 cup fresh parsley, chopped
- 1/4 cup fresh oregano leaves, chopped (or 1 teaspoon dried oregano)
- Salt and freshly ground black pepper, to taste

For the Dressing:

- 1/4 cup extra-virgin olive oil
- 3 tablespoons red wine vinegar
- 1 teaspoon Dijon mustard
- 1 clove garlic, minced
- 1/2 teaspoon dried oregano
- Salt and freshly ground black pepper, to taste

Instructions:

1- In a large bowl, combine the diced tomatoes, cucumber, and green bell pepper.
2- Add the Kalamata olives, crumbled feta cheese, chopped fresh parsley, and chopped fresh oregano to the bowl.
3- In a separate small bowl, whisk together the extra-virgin olive oil, red wine vinegar, Dijon mustard, minced garlic, and dried oregano to make the dressing. Season the dressing with salt and freshly ground black pepper to taste.
4- Pour the dressing over the salad ingredients in the large bowl. Gently toss the salad to ensure all the ingredients are coated with the dressing.
5- Taste the salad and adjust the seasoning with additional salt, pepper, or dried oregano as needed.
6- Let the Greek salad sit for about 15-20 minutes to allow the flavors to meld and the vegetables to marinate.

7- Just before serving, give the salad a final gentle toss to redistribute the dressing and ingredients.

8- Serve the onion-free Greek salad as a refreshing and vibrant appetizer or side dish. It pairs well with grilled meats, seafood, or as part of a Mediterranean-inspired meal.

Note: This onion-free Greek salad showcases the colorful and vibrant flavors of the Mediterranean without the use of onions. The combination of fresh vegetables, olives, and feta cheese is complemented by a simple yet flavorful dressing. Customize the salad by adjusting the quantities of ingredients and dressing according to your preference. Enjoy the light and zesty taste of this classic dish.

2.3. Avocado Cilantro Lime Dressing (Onion-Free)

Yield: Approximately 1 cup

Ingredients:

- 1 ripe avocado, peeled and pitted
- 1/4 cup fresh cilantro leaves, chopped
- 1/4 cup plain Greek yogurt
- 2 tablespoons fresh lime juice
- 2 tablespoons extra-virgin olive oil
- 1 clove garlic, minced
- 1/2 teaspoon ground cumin
- Salt and freshly ground black pepper, to taste

Instructions:

1- In a food processor or blender, combine the ripe avocado, chopped cilantro leaves, plain Greek yogurt, fresh lime juice, extra-virgin olive oil, minced garlic, and ground cumin.

2- Blend the ingredients until smooth and creamy, scraping down the sides of the bowl as needed. If the mixture is too thick, you can add a little water or more lime juice to achieve your desired consistency.

3- Taste the dressing and season with salt and freshly ground black pepper according to your preference. Adjust the lime juice or other seasonings if needed.

4- Once the dressing is smooth and well-seasoned, transfer it to a glass jar or container with a tight-fitting lid.

5- Store the avocado cilantro lime dressing in the refrigerator for at least 30 minutes to allow the flavors to meld and develop. The dressing can be stored for up to 3-4 days.
6- Before using, give the dressing a good shake or stir to ensure it's well mixed.
7- Serve the onion-free avocado cilantro lime dressing as a versatile and flavorful accompaniment to salads, grilled vegetables, roasted meats, or as a dip for fresh veggies.

Note: This creamy avocado cilantro lime dressing offers a refreshing burst of flavor without the use of onions. The combination of avocado, cilantro, lime, and Greek yogurt creates a luscious and tangy dressing that's perfect for a variety of dishes. Adjust the seasonings and consistency to suit your taste. Drizzle it generously over your favorite salads and enjoy the zesty goodness.

2.4. Creamy Dijon Vinaigrette (Onion-Free)

Yield: Approximately 1/2 cup

Ingredients:

- 3 tablespoons extra-virgin olive oil
- 2 tablespoons Dijon mustard
- 2 tablespoons plain Greek yogurt
- 2 tablespoons red wine vinegar
- 1 tablespoon honey or maple syrup
- 1 clove garlic, minced
- 1/2 teaspoon dried thyme
- Salt and freshly ground black pepper, to taste

Instructions:

1- In a small bowl, whisk together the Dijon mustard, plain Greek yogurt, red wine vinegar, and honey (or maple syrup) until well combined.
2- Slowly drizzle in the extra-virgin olive oil while continuously whisking to emulsify the dressing.
3- Add the minced garlic and dried thyme to the bowl. Continue whisking until all the ingredients are thoroughly blended.

4- Taste the dressing and season with salt and freshly ground black pepper according to your preference. Adjust the honey or maple syrup for sweetness and the vinegar for tanginess, if needed.

5- Once the creamy Dijon vinaigrette is well mixed and seasoned, transfer it to a glass jar or container with a tight-fitting lid.

6- Store the dressing in the refrigerator for at least 30 minutes to allow the flavors to meld and develop. The dressing can be stored for up to 5-7 days.

7- Before using, give the dressing a good shake or stir to ensure it's well combined.

8- Drizzle the onion-free creamy Dijon vinaigrette over your favorite salads, roasted vegetables, or grilled proteins to add a tangy and luscious touch.

Note: This creamy Dijon vinaigrette provides a delightful balance of tanginess and creaminess without the use of onions. The Dijon mustard and Greek yogurt create a velvety texture, while the honey adds a touch of sweetness. Adjust the seasonings and consistency to your liking. Elevate your dishes with the rich and flavorful taste of this versatile dressing.

2.5. Mango and Basil Salad (Onion-Free)

Servings: 4

Ingredients:

- 2 ripe mangoes, peeled, pitted, and diced
- 1 cup cherry tomatoes, halved
- 1/2 English cucumber, diced
- 1/4 cup fresh basil leaves, torn
- 2 tablespoons crumbled feta cheese (optional)
- 2 tablespoons chopped toasted almonds or walnuts
- Juice of 1 lime
- 2 tablespoons extra-virgin olive oil
- 1 teaspoon honey or maple syrup
- Salt and freshly ground black pepper, to taste

Instructions:

1- In a large mixing bowl, combine the diced mangoes, halved cherry tomatoes, diced cucumber, and torn basil leaves.

2- If using, sprinkle the crumbled feta cheese over the salad.
3- In a small bowl, whisk together the lime juice, extra-virgin olive oil, honey (or maple syrup), salt, and freshly ground black pepper to create the dressing.
4- Drizzle the dressing over the mango and basil salad.
Gently toss the salad to ensure that the ingredients are evenly coated with the dressing.
5- Taste the salad and adjust the seasonings, lime juice, or honey to your liking.
6- Just before serving, sprinkle the chopped toasted almonds or walnuts over the salad for a delightful crunch.
7- Serve the onion-free mango and basil salad as a refreshing and colorful appetizer or side dish. It pairs well with grilled chicken, seafood, or as part of a light and vibrant meal.

Note: This onion-free mango and basil salad showcases the sweetness of ripe mangoes and the aromatic freshness of basil without the use of onions. The combination of flavors and textures is enhanced by the zesty lime dressing and the optional addition of crumbled feta cheese and toasted nuts. Customize the salad by adjusting the quantities of ingredients and dressing according to your preference. Enjoy the tropical and herbaceous flavors of this delicious dish.

3.1. Lemon Herb Roast Chicken (Onion-Free)

Servings: 4-6

Ingredients:

- 1 whole chicken (approximately 4-5 pounds)
- 2 lemons, divided (1 for juice and 1 for roasting)
- 4 cloves garlic, minced
- 2 tablespoons fresh rosemary leaves, chopped
- 2 tablespoons fresh thyme leaves, chopped
- 2 tablespoons fresh parsley, chopped
- 1/4 cup extra-virgin olive oil
- Salt and freshly ground black pepper, to taste
- 1 cup chicken broth or white wine (for roasting)

Instructions:

1- Preheat your oven to 425°F (220°C).

2- Rinse the whole chicken under cold water and pat it dry with paper towels.

3- In a small bowl, combine the minced garlic, chopped rosemary, chopped thyme, chopped parsley, extra-virgin olive oil, and the juice of 1 lemon. Mix well to create the herb and garlic mixture.

4- Gently separate the skin from the chicken breasts and thighs, being careful not to tear the skin.

5- Rub the herb and garlic mixture under the skin, massaging it onto the meat to evenly distribute the flavors.

6- Cut the second lemon into quarters and stuff the chicken cavity with the lemon quarters.

7- Tie the chicken legs together with kitchen twine to help maintain its shape during roasting.

8- Place the seasoned chicken on a roasting rack in a roasting pan or on a baking sheet.

9- Season the outside of the chicken with salt and freshly ground black pepper.

10- Pour the chicken broth or white wine into the bottom of the roasting pan.

11- Roast the chicken in the preheated oven for about 1 to 1.5 hours, or until the internal temperature of the thickest part of the thigh reaches 165°F (74°C) and the juices run clear when pierced with a fork.

12- If the chicken starts to brown too quickly, you can cover it loosely with aluminum foil.

13- Once the chicken is cooked, remove it from the oven and let it rest for about 10-15 minutes before carving.

14- Carve the lemon herb roast chicken into serving portions and arrange them on a platter.

15- Serve the succulent and flavorful onion-free lemon herb roast chicken alongside your favorite sides and enjoy a comforting and satisfying meal.

Note: This lemon herb roast chicken is a classic dish with a burst of citrusy and aromatic flavors. The blend of fresh herbs and lemon infuses the chicken with a delightful taste. Customize the seasoning and roasting time based on your preferences and the size of the chicken. Savor the juicy and tender meat of this flavorful roast.

3.2. Beef Stroganoff (Onion-Free)

Servings: 4-6

Ingredients:

- 1 pound beef sirloin or tenderloin, thinly sliced into strips
- 2 cloves garlic, minced
- 8 ounces white mushrooms, sliced
- 2 tablespoons unsalted butter
- 1 tablespoon all-purpose flour
- 1 cup beef broth
- 1 tablespoon Dijon mustard
- 1 cup sour cream
- Salt and freshly ground black pepper, to taste
- 2 tablespoons fresh parsley, chopped
- 8 ounces egg noodles, cooked according to package instructions

Instructions:

1- In a large skillet, melt 1 tablespoon of butter over medium-high heat. Add the sliced beef and cook for 2-3 minutes until browned. Remove the beef from the skillet and set aside.

2- In the same skillet, add the remaining tablespoon of butter. Add the minced garlic and sliced mushrooms. Sauté for about 5-7 minutes, until the mushrooms are cooked and any liquid has evaporated.

3- Sprinkle the flour over the mushrooms and stir well to combine. Cook for 1-2 minutes to remove the raw flour taste.

4- Slowly pour in the beef broth while stirring to create a smooth sauce. Bring the mixture to a simmer and let it cook for 2-3 minutes, allowing the sauce to thicken.

5- Stir in the Dijon mustard and sour cream, combining well with the sauce. Cook for an additional 2-3 minutes to heat through.

6- Return the cooked beef to the skillet and mix it into the sauce. Let the beef simmer in the sauce for another 2-3 minutes.

7- Taste the beef stroganoff and season with salt and freshly ground black pepper according to your preference.

8- Just before serving, stir in the chopped fresh parsley for a burst of color and freshness.

9- Serve the onion-free beef stroganoff over cooked egg noodles, rice, or mashed potatoes.

Note: This onion-free beef stroganoff is a comforting and hearty dish that's perfect for a satisfying meal. The combination of tender beef, creamy sauce, and mushrooms creates a rich and flavorful experience. Adjust the seasonings and consistency of the sauce to your liking. Enjoy this classic dish alongside your favorite side and savor the warm and indulgent flavors.

3.3. Grilled Herb-Marinated Salmon (Onion-Free)

Servings: 4

Ingredients:

- 4 salmon fillets (6-8 ounces each)
- 3 tablespoons fresh lemon juice
- 3 tablespoons extra-virgin olive oil
- 2 cloves garlic, minced
- 2 tablespoons fresh parsley, chopped
- 1 tablespoon fresh dill, chopped
- 1 teaspoon fresh rosemary leaves, chopped
- 1 teaspoon fresh thyme leaves, chopped
- Salt and freshly ground black pepper, to taste

- Lemon wedges, for serving

Instructions:

1- In a bowl, whisk together the fresh lemon juice, extra-virgin olive oil, minced garlic, chopped parsley, chopped dill, chopped rosemary, and chopped thyme to create the marinade.

2- Place the salmon fillets in a shallow dish or resealable plastic bag.

3- Pour the marinade over the salmon, making sure each fillet is well coated. Seal the dish or bag and refrigerate for at least 30 minutes to marinate. For optimal flavor, you can marinate the salmon for up to 2 hours.

4- Preheat the grill to medium-high heat. Make sure the grill grates are clean and well-oiled to prevent sticking.

5- Remove the salmon fillets from the marinade and shake off any excess liquid.

6- Season the salmon fillets with salt and freshly ground black pepper.

7- Place the salmon fillets on the preheated grill, skin-side down. Cook for about 4-5 minutes on the first side.

8- Carefully flip the salmon fillets using a spatula, and continue to grill for an additional 4-5 minutes on the second side, or until the salmon flakes easily with a fork.

9- Remove the grilled herb-marinated salmon from the grill and transfer to serving plates.

10- Serve the salmon fillets with lemon wedges on the side for an extra zesty kick.

11- Enjoy the onion-free grilled herb-marinated salmon with your choice of side dishes, such as steamed vegetables, quinoa, or a fresh salad.

Note: This grilled herb-marinated salmon offers a burst of fresh herb flavors without the use of onions. The marinade enhances the natural taste of the salmon, creating a delightful and aromatic dish. Adjust the grilling time based on the thickness of the salmon fillets and your preferred level of doneness. Serve this delicious and nutritious meal for a satisfying and wholesome dining experience.

3.4. Mushroom and Spinach Stuffed Bell Peppers (Onion-Free)

Servings: 4

Ingredients:

- 4 large bell peppers, any color
- 8 ounces mushrooms, finely chopped
- 2 cups fresh spinach, chopped
- 2 cloves garlic, minced
- 1 cup cooked quinoa or rice
- 1 cup shredded mozzarella cheese, divided
- 1/4 cup grated Parmesan cheese
- 1 tablespoon olive oil
- 1 teaspoon dried oregano
- 1 teaspoon dried thyme
- Salt and freshly ground black pepper, to taste

Instructions:

1- Preheat the oven to 375°F (190°C).
2- Cut the tops off the bell peppers and remove the seeds and membranes. If needed, slightly trim the bottoms of the peppers to help them stand upright.
3- In a large skillet, heat the olive oil over medium heat. Add the chopped mushrooms and sauté for about 5-7 minutes, until they release their moisture and start to brown.
4- Add the minced garlic and sauté for an additional 1-2 minutes, until fragrant.
5- Stir in the chopped spinach and cook until wilted, about 2-3 minutes.
6- Remove the skillet from the heat and stir in the cooked quinoa or rice, half of the shredded mozzarella cheese, grated Parmesan cheese, dried oregano, dried thyme, salt, and freshly ground black pepper. Mix well to combine.
7- Carefully spoon the mushroom and spinach mixture into the hollowed-out bell peppers, pressing down gently to pack the filling.
8- Place the stuffed bell peppers in a baking dish and cover the dish with aluminum foil.
9- Bake the stuffed bell peppers in the preheated oven for about 25-30 minutes, or until the peppers are tender.
10- Remove the foil and sprinkle the remaining shredded mozzarella cheese over the tops of the peppers.
11- Return the peppers to the oven and bake for an additional 5-7 minutes, or until the cheese is melted and bubbly.
12- Once cooked, remove the stuffed bell peppers from the oven and let them cool slightly before serving.
13- Serve the mushroom and spinach stuffed bell peppers as a satisfying and flavorful main dish, accompanied by a fresh salad or your favorite side.

Note: These onion-free mushroom and spinach stuffed bell peppers are a wholesome and delicious option for a satisfying meal. The combination of savory mushrooms, vibrant spinach, and cheesy goodness creates a delightful filling for the bell peppers. Customize the ingredients and seasonings to your liking. Enjoy the hearty and nutritious flavors of this comforting dish.

3.5. Eggplant Parmesan (Onion-Free)

Servings: 4-6

Ingredients:

For the Eggplant:

- 2 medium eggplants, sliced into 1/2-inch rounds
- Salt, for sweating
- 1 cup all-purpose flour
- 3 large eggs
- 2 cups breadcrumbs (preferably Italian-style)
- 1 cup grated Parmesan cheese
- Olive oil, for frying

For the Assembly:

- 2 cups marinara sauce (homemade or store-bought)
- 2 cups shredded mozzarella cheese
- 1/4 cup fresh basil leaves, torn
- 1/4 cup grated Parmesan cheese
- Salt and freshly ground black pepper, to taste

Instructions:

1- Place the eggplant slices on a baking sheet and sprinkle both sides with salt.
2- Allow the eggplant to sit for about 30 minutes to draw out excess moisture. After 30 minutes, pat the eggplant slices dry with paper towels.
3- Preheat the oven to 375°F (190°C).
4- Set up a breading station: In one shallow dish, place the flour. In another shallow dish, beat the eggs. In a third shallow dish, combine the breadcrumbs and grated Parmesan cheese.

5- Dredge each eggplant slice in the flour, then dip it into the beaten eggs, and coat it with the breadcrumb mixture. Press the breadcrumbs onto the eggplant to adhere.

6- In a large skillet, heat enough olive oil to cover the bottom of the pan over medium-high heat. Fry the breaded eggplant slices in batches, cooking until golden brown on both sides, about 3-4 minutes per side. Place the cooked eggplant slices on paper towels to drain excess oil.

7- In a baking dish, spread a thin layer of marinara sauce on the bottom.

8- Place a layer of fried eggplant slices on top of the sauce.

9- Spoon more marinara sauce over the eggplant slices, followed by a layer of shredded mozzarella cheese, torn basil leaves, and grated Parmesan cheese. Season with salt and freshly ground black pepper.

10- Repeat the layers, finishing with a final layer of marinara sauce, mozzarella cheese, torn basil, and grated Parmesan.

11- Cover the baking dish with aluminum foil and bake in the preheated oven for about 25-30 minutes, or until the cheese is melted and bubbly.

12- Remove the foil and continue baking for an additional 10-15 minutes, until the top is golden brown and crispy.

13- Once cooked, remove the eggplant Parmesan from the oven and let it cool slightly before serving.

14- Serve the onion-free eggplant Parmesan as a hearty and flavorful main dish, accompanied by a side of pasta, a fresh salad, or crusty bread.

Note: This onion-free eggplant Parmesan features layers of crispy breaded eggplant slices, tangy marinara sauce, and gooey melted cheese. The absence of onions allows the flavors of the eggplant and cheese to shine. Customize the recipe by adjusting the seasonings, cheese, and sauce to your liking. Enjoy the comforting and savory taste of this classic Italian dish.

4.1. Creamy Pesto Pasta (Onion-Free)

Servings: 4-6

Ingredients:

- 12 ounces pasta (such as fettuccine, linguine, or penne)
- 1 cup fresh basil leaves
- 1/2 cup grated Parmesan cheese
- 1/4 cup pine nuts or walnuts
- 2 cloves garlic, minced
- 1/2 cup extra-virgin olive oil
- 1/2 cup heavy cream
- Salt and freshly ground black pepper, to taste
- Grated Parmesan cheese, for serving
- Fresh basil leaves, for garnish

Instructions:

1- Cook the pasta according to the package instructions until al dente. Drain and set aside.

2- In a food processor, combine the fresh basil leaves, grated Parmesan cheese, pine nuts or walnuts, and minced garlic.

3- Pulse the mixture until the ingredients are finely chopped and well combined.

4- With the food processor running, slowly drizzle in the extra-virgin olive oil until a smooth pesto sauce forms.

5- In a separate saucepan, heat the heavy cream over medium-low heat until warmed through. Do not let it come to a boil.

6- Stir the prepared pesto sauce into the warmed heavy cream. Mix well to combine.

7- Season the creamy pesto sauce with salt and freshly ground black pepper to taste. Keep in mind that the Parmesan cheese in the pesto adds some saltiness.

8- In a large mixing bowl, toss the cooked pasta with the creamy pesto sauce until the pasta is coated evenly.

9- Serve the creamy pesto pasta in individual dishes, garnished with additional grated Parmesan cheese and fresh basil leaves.

10- Enjoy the onion-free creamy pesto pasta as a comforting and flavorful main dish. Serve it with a side of garlic bread, a simple salad, or steamed vegetables.

Note: This onion-free creamy pesto pasta offers a luscious and aromatic combination of fresh basil, Parmesan cheese, and nuts. The creamy sauce adds a velvety texture to the pasta without the use of onions. Customize the dish by adjusting the consistency of the sauce, the amount of cheese, and the type of pasta used. Indulge in the rich and satisfying flavors of this creamy and herbaceous pasta.

4.2. Mushroom Risotto (Onion-Free)

Servings: 4-6

Ingredients:

- 2 cups Arborio rice
- 8 ounces mushrooms, sliced (such as cremini or button mushrooms)
- 4 cups vegetable or chicken broth, kept warm
- 1/2 cup dry white wine
- 3 tablespoons unsalted butter
- 2 cloves garlic, minced
- 1/2 cup grated Parmesan cheese
- 2 tablespoons fresh parsley, chopped
- Salt and freshly ground black pepper, to taste

Instructions:

1- In a large skillet or wide saucepan, melt 2 tablespoons of butter over medium heat.

2- Add the sliced mushrooms to the skillet and cook until they release their moisture and start to brown, about 5-7 minutes. Remove the mushrooms from the skillet and set them aside.

3- In the same skillet, add the Arborio rice and minced garlic. Sauté for about 1-2 minutes until the rice is lightly toasted and the garlic is fragrant.

4- Pour in the dry white wine and cook, stirring, until most of the wine has been absorbed by the rice.

5- Begin adding the warm broth to the rice, one ladleful at a time. Stir constantly and allow each ladleful of broth to be absorbed before adding the next. Continue this process until the rice is creamy and cooked to your desired level of tenderness. This usually takes about 18-20 minutes.

6- Stir in the cooked mushrooms during the last few minutes of cooking.

7- Once the rice is cooked and creamy, remove the skillet from the heat. Stir in the remaining tablespoon of butter and grated Parmesan cheese until well incorporated.

8- Season the mushroom risotto with salt and freshly ground black pepper to taste.

9- Divide the mushroom risotto among serving plates and garnish with chopped fresh parsley.

10- Serve the onion-free mushroom risotto as a comforting and flavorful main dish. Enjoy it with a side of steamed vegetables, a green salad, or crusty bread.

Note: This onion-free mushroom risotto features rich and earthy flavors from the mushrooms, and the creamy texture of Arborio rice is achieved without the use of onions. Customize the recipe by using your favorite type of mushrooms and adjusting the seasonings to your taste. Savor the luxurious and velvety goodness of this classic Italian dish.

4.3. Spinach and Ricotta Stuffed Shells (Onion-Free)

Servings: 4-6

Ingredients:

For the Stuffed Shells:

- 20 jumbo pasta shells
- 10 ounces fresh spinach, cooked and chopped
- 15 ounces ricotta cheese
- 1 cup shredded mozzarella cheese
- 1/2 cup grated Parmesan cheese
- 2 cloves garlic, minced
- 1 teaspoon dried basil
- 1 teaspoon dried oregano
- Salt and freshly ground black pepper, to taste

For the Tomato Sauce:

- 2 cups marinara sauce (homemade or store-bought)
- 1 teaspoon dried Italian herbs (such as basil, oregano, and thyme)
- Salt and freshly ground black pepper, to taste

Instructions:

1- Preheat the oven to 375°F (190°C).
2- Cook the jumbo pasta shells according to the package instructions until al dente. Drain and set aside.
3- In a large mixing bowl, combine the cooked and chopped spinach, ricotta cheese, shredded mozzarella cheese, grated Parmesan cheese, minced garlic, dried basil, dried oregano, salt, and freshly ground black pepper. Mix well to create the stuffing mixture.
4- In a separate bowl, mix together the marinara sauce, dried Italian herbs, salt, and freshly ground black pepper to create the tomato sauce.
5- Spoon a thin layer of tomato sauce onto the bottom of a baking dish.
6- Carefully stuff each jumbo pasta shell with the spinach and ricotta mixture and place them in the baking dish.
7- Once all the shells are stuffed and arranged in the baking dish, pour the remaining tomato sauce over the top, covering the shells evenly.
8- Cover the baking dish with aluminum foil and bake in the preheated oven for about 25-30 minutes, or until the cheese is melted and bubbly.
9- Remove the foil and continue baking for an additional 10-15 minutes, or until the top is golden brown and crispy.
10- Once cooked, remove the spinach and ricotta stuffed shells from the oven and let them cool slightly before serving.
11- Serve the onion-free spinach and ricotta stuffed shells as a hearty and flavorful main dish. Pair them with a side salad, garlic bread, or steamed vegetables.

Note: These onion-free spinach and ricotta stuffed shells offer a delightful combination of creamy cheese, spinach, and aromatic herbs. The tomato sauce adds a burst of flavor to the dish without the use of onions. Customize the recipe by adjusting the seasonings, cheese, and sauce according to your taste. Enjoy the comforting and satisfying taste of this classic Italian dish.

4.4. Lemon Garlic Shrimp Linguine (Onion-Free)

Servings: 4

Ingredients:

- 12 ounces linguine pasta

- 1 pound large shrimp, peeled and deveined
- 4 tablespoons unsalted butter
- 4 cloves garlic, minced
- Zest and juice of 1 lemon
- 1/4 teaspoon red pepper flakes (optional)
- Salt and freshly ground black pepper, to taste
- 2 tablespoons fresh parsley, chopped
- Grated Parmesan cheese, for serving

Instructions:

1- Cook the linguine pasta according to the package instructions until al dente. Drain and set aside.

2- In a large skillet, melt 2 tablespoons of butter over medium heat.

3- Add the minced garlic to the skillet and sauté for about 1-2 minutes until fragrant. Be careful not to let the garlic brown.

4- Add the shrimp to the skillet and cook for about 2-3 minutes on each side, or until they turn pink and opaque.

5- Remove the shrimp from the skillet and set them aside.

6- In the same skillet, add the remaining 2 tablespoons of butter. Allow it to melt and mix with any residual garlic and shrimp flavors.

7- Stir in the lemon zest, lemon juice, and red pepper flakes (if using) into the butter. Season with salt and freshly ground black pepper to taste.

8- Add the cooked linguine to the skillet and toss to coat the pasta with the lemon garlic butter.

9- Gently stir in the cooked shrimp, making sure they are evenly distributed throughout the pasta.

10- Taste the linguine and adjust the seasoning, lemon juice, or red pepper flakes according to your preference.

11- Just before serving, sprinkle the chopped fresh parsley over the lemon garlic shrimp linguine.

12- Serve the onion-free lemon garlic shrimp linguine as a zesty and flavorful main dish. Garnish with grated Parmesan cheese and enjoy!

Note: This onion-free lemon garlic shrimp linguine is a light and refreshing pasta dish with a burst of citrus and garlic flavors. The succulent shrimp and tangy lemon create a delightful combination that's perfect for a satisfying meal. Customize the recipe by adjusting the amount of garlic, lemon, or red pepper flakes to your liking. Savor the simple and delicious taste of this classic dish.

4.5. Thai Peanut Noodles (Onion-Free)

Servings: 4

Ingredients:

For the Peanut Sauce:

- 1/2 cup creamy peanut butter
- 1/4 cup low-sodium soy sauce
- 3 tablespoons fresh lime juice
- 2 tablespoons honey or maple syrup
- 2 tablespoons rice vinegar
- 2 cloves garlic, minced
- 1 teaspoon grated fresh ginger
- 1/4 teaspoon red pepper flakes (adjust to taste)
- 1/4 cup warm water (or more, as needed)

For the Noodles:

- 8 ounces rice noodles (pad Thai noodles)
- 1 cup shredded carrots
- 1 cup red bell pepper, julienned
- 1 cup cucumber, julienned
- 1/4 cup chopped fresh cilantro
- 1/4 cup chopped roasted peanuts
- Lime wedges, for serving

Instructions:

1- In a bowl, whisk together all the ingredients for the peanut sauce until smooth.
2- Add warm water gradually to achieve the desired consistency. Set aside.
3- Cook the rice noodles according to the package instructions until al dente. Drain and rinse with cold water to stop the cooking process.
4- In a large bowl, toss the cooked rice noodles with the shredded carrots, red bell pepper, and cucumber.
5- Pour the prepared peanut sauce over the noodles and vegetables. Toss well to ensure even coating.
6- Divide the Thai peanut noodles among serving plates.

7- Garnish the noodles with chopped fresh cilantro and roasted peanuts.
8- Serve the onion-free Thai peanut noodles with lime wedges on the side.
Squeeze lime juice over the noodles just before eating to enhance the flavors.
9- Enjoy the vibrant and flavorful Thai peanut noodles as a satisfying and
delicious dish. Customize the ingredients and adjust the level of spiciness to suit
your taste.

Note: This onion-free Thai peanut noodles recipe features a luscious and nutty peanut
sauce combined with fresh vegetables and rice noodles. The absence of onions allows
the other ingredients to shine, creating a delightful and satisfying dish. Feel free to add
cooked chicken, shrimp, or tofu for added protein. Enjoy the harmonious blend of sweet,
tangy, and savory flavors in this classic Thai-inspired dish.

5.1. Roasted Garlic Mashed Potatoes (Onion-Free)

Servings: 4-6

Ingredients:

- 2 pounds Russet or Yukon Gold potatoes, peeled and cut into chunks
- 1 head of garlic
- 1/4 cup unsalted butter, softened
- 1/2 cup milk or cream (adjust to desired consistency)
- Salt and freshly ground black pepper, to taste
- Chopped fresh chives or parsley, for garnish

Instructions:

1- Preheat the oven to 400°F (200°C).

2- Cut the top off the head of garlic to expose the cloves. Place the garlic on a piece of aluminum foil and drizzle it with a little olive oil. Wrap the garlic in the foil and roast in the preheated oven for about 30-35 minutes, or until the garlic cloves are soft and golden brown. Remove from the oven and let it cool slightly.

3- While the garlic is roasting, place the peeled and cut potatoes in a large pot. Cover them with cold water and add a generous pinch of salt. Bring the water to a boil, then reduce the heat to a simmer. Cook the potatoes until they are fork-tender, about 15-20 minutes.

4- Drain the cooked potatoes and return them to the pot.

5- Squeeze the roasted garlic cloves out of the skins and add them to the pot with the potatoes.

6- Add the softened butter and milk or cream to the pot.

7- Use a potato masher or a hand mixer to mash the potatoes, roasted garlic, butter, and milk until smooth and creamy. Add more milk or cream as needed to reach your desired consistency.

8- Season the mashed potatoes with salt and freshly ground black pepper to taste. Mix well to combine.

9- Transfer the roasted garlic mashed potatoes to a serving dish.

10- Garnish the mashed potatoes with chopped fresh chives or parsley for added flavor and color.

11- Serve the onion-free roasted garlic mashed potatoes as a comforting and flavorful side dish. Enjoy them with roasted meats, grilled vegetables, or your favorite main course.

Note: These onion-free roasted garlic mashed potatoes offer a rich and velvety texture with a delightful roasted garlic flavor. The absence of onions allows the roasted garlic to take center stage in this classic side dish. Customize the recipe by adjusting the amount of butter, milk, or cream to your preference. Indulge in the creamy and savory taste of this comforting dish that pairs perfectly with a variety of meals.

5.2. Lemon Herb Quinoa (Onion-Free)

Servings: 4-6

Ingredients:

- 1 cup quinoa, rinsed and drained
- 2 cups vegetable or chicken broth (or water)
- Zest and juice of 1 lemon
- 2 tablespoons fresh parsley, chopped
- 1 tablespoon fresh thyme leaves, chopped
- 1 tablespoon fresh chives, chopped
- 2 tablespoons extra-virgin olive oil
- Salt and freshly ground black pepper, to taste

Instructions:

1- In a medium saucepan, combine the rinsed quinoa and vegetable or chicken broth (or water). Bring to a boil.
2- Reduce the heat to low, cover the saucepan with a lid, and simmer for about 15-20 minutes, or until the quinoa is cooked and the liquid is absorbed. Fluff the quinoa with a fork.
3- In a bowl, whisk together the lemon zest, lemon juice, chopped parsley, chopped thyme, and chopped chives.
4- Gradually drizzle in the extra-virgin olive oil while whisking to create a flavorful dressing.
5- Pour the lemon herb dressing over the cooked quinoa and toss to combine.
6- Season the lemon herb quinoa with salt and freshly ground black pepper to taste. Mix well to distribute the flavors.
7- Serve the onion-free lemon herb quinoa as a refreshing and aromatic side dish. Enjoy it alongside grilled chicken, fish, or roasted vegetables.

Note: This onion-free lemon herb quinoa showcases the bright and zesty flavors of lemon combined with fresh herbs. The quinoa provides a nutty and nutritious base for the dish. Customize the recipe by adjusting the types of herbs used and the level of lemon zest and juice. Embrace the light and invigorating taste of this versatile and wholesome side dish.

5.3. Honey Glazed Carrots (Onion-Free)

Servings: 4-6

Ingredients:

- 1 pound carrots, peeled and sliced into rounds or sticks
- 2 tablespoons unsalted butter
- 2 tablespoons honey
- 1 teaspoon fresh thyme leaves (optional)
- Salt and freshly ground black pepper, to taste
- Chopped fresh parsley, for garnish

Instructions:

1- In a medium saucepan, melt the butter over medium heat.
2- Add the sliced carrots to the saucepan and sauté for about 3-4 minutes, stirring occasionally.
3- Drizzle the honey over the carrots and stir to coat them evenly.
4- If using, sprinkle the fresh thyme leaves over the carrots.
5- Season the carrots with salt and freshly ground black pepper to taste. Mix well.
6- Reduce the heat to low, cover the saucepan with a lid, and let the carrots simmer for about 10-15 minutes, or until they are tender. Stir occasionally.
7- Once the carrots are cooked to your desired tenderness, remove the lid and continue to cook for a few more minutes to allow the glaze to thicken.
8- Transfer the honey glazed carrots to a serving dish.
9- Garnish the carrots with chopped fresh parsley for added color and flavor.
10- Serve the onion-free honey glazed carrots as a delectable and sweet side dish. Enjoy them alongside roasted meats, grilled poultry, or a variety of main courses.

Note: These onion-free honey glazed carrots offer a delightful combination of sweetness and buttery richness. The simple and elegant glaze enhances the natural flavors of the carrots without the use of onions. Customize the recipe by adjusting the amount of honey and butter to your liking. Savor the tender and flavorful taste of this classic side dish that's perfect for any meal.

5.4. Grilled Asparagus with Balsamic Glaze (Onion-Free)

Servings: 4-6

Ingredients:

- 1 bunch fresh asparagus spears, tough ends trimmed
- 2 tablespoons extra-virgin olive oil
- Salt and freshly ground black pepper, to taste
- 1/4 cup balsamic vinegar
- 2 tablespoons honey or maple syrup
- 1 teaspoon Dijon mustard
- Chopped fresh parsley, for garnish

Instructions:

1- Preheat the grill to medium-high heat.
2- In a bowl, toss the trimmed asparagus spears with extra-virgin olive oil, salt, and freshly ground black pepper until evenly coated.
3- Place the asparagus on the grill grates in a single layer. Grill for about 3-4 minutes, turning occasionally, until the asparagus is tender and has grill marks.
4- While the asparagus is grilling, prepare the balsamic glaze. In a small saucepan, combine the balsamic vinegar, honey or maple syrup, and Dijon mustard.
5- Bring the mixture to a simmer over medium heat. Cook for about 5-7 minutes, stirring occasionally, until the glaze has thickened and reduced by about half.
6- Remove the balsamic glaze from the heat and let it cool slightly. It will continue to thicken as it cools.
7- Arrange the grilled asparagus on a serving platter.
8- Drizzle the balsamic glaze over the grilled asparagus.
9- Garnish the dish with chopped fresh parsley for added flavor and color.
10- Serve the onion-free grilled asparagus with balsamic glaze as a vibrant and elegant side dish. Enjoy it alongside grilled meats, seafood, or your favorite main course.

Note: This onion-free grilled asparagus with balsamic glaze offers a harmonious blend of smoky grilled flavors and sweet tangy glaze. The balsamic reduction enhances the taste of the asparagus without the use of onions. Customize the recipe by adjusting the sweetness of the glaze to your preference. Embrace the simple and delightful taste of this seasonal and nutritious side dish.

5.5. Cucumber and Mint Raita (Onion-Free)

Servings: 4-6

Ingredients:

- 2 cups plain yogurt (Greek yogurt or regular yogurt)
- 1 cup cucumber, peeled, seeded, and finely chopped
- 2 tablespoons fresh mint leaves, finely chopped
- 1 teaspoon ground cumin
- 1/2 teaspoon ground coriander
- 1/4 teaspoon ground paprika (optional, for color)
- Salt, to taste
- Freshly ground black pepper, to taste
- 1/4 teaspoon roasted cumin powder (for garnish)
- Fresh mint leaves, for garnish

Instructions:

1- In a mixing bowl, whisk the plain yogurt until smooth and creamy.
2- Add the finely chopped cucumber and fresh mint leaves to the yogurt. Mix well to combine.
3- Stir in the ground cumin, ground coriander, ground paprika (if using), salt, and freshly ground black pepper. Adjust the seasonings to your taste.
4- Chill the cucumber and mint raita in the refrigerator for at least 30 minutes to allow the flavors to meld.
5- Before serving, sprinkle a pinch of roasted cumin powder over the raita for extra flavor and aroma.
6- Garnish the raita with a few fresh mint leaves.
7- Serve the onion-free cucumber and mint raita as a refreshing and cooling side dish. It complements a variety of Indian and Middle Eastern dishes, such as biryani, kebabs, or curries.

Note: This onion-free cucumber and mint raita is a creamy and tangy accompaniment that adds a burst of freshness to your meals. The combination of cool cucumber and fragrant mint creates a delightful balance of flavors. Customize the recipe by adjusting the herbs and spices to your preference. Enjoy the cooling and soothing taste of this classic yogurt-based condiment.

6.1. Rosemary Focaccia (Onion-Free)

Yield: 1 large focaccia

Ingredients:

For the Dough:

- 3 1/2 cups all-purpose flour
- 2 teaspoons active dry yeast
- 1 1/4 cups warm water
- 1 teaspoon sugar
- 1 teaspoon salt
- 3 tablespoons olive oil

For the Topping:

- 2-3 sprigs fresh rosemary
- Coarse sea salt, for sprinkling
- Extra-virgin olive oil, for drizzling

Instructions:

1- In a small bowl, combine the warm water, sugar, and active dry yeast. Let it sit for about 5-10 minutes, or until the mixture becomes frothy.

2- In a large mixing bowl, combine the flour and salt. Make a well in the center.

3- Pour the yeast mixture and olive oil into the well. Mix the ingredients together until a dough forms.

4- Turn the dough out onto a floured surface and knead it for about 5-7 minutes, or until it becomes smooth and elastic.

5- Place the dough in a lightly oiled bowl, cover it with a damp cloth, and let it rise in a warm place for about 1 hour, or until it has doubled in size.

6- Preheat the oven to 400°F (200°C).

7- Punch down the risen dough and turn it out onto a baking sheet lined with parchment paper.

8- Gently stretch and press the dough to fit the baking sheet, creating an even layer.

9- Cover the dough with a damp cloth and let it rest for about 15-20 minutes.

10- After resting, use your fingertips to create dimples all over the surface of the dough.

11- Drizzle a generous amount of olive oil over the dough, allowing it to pool in the dimples.

12- Strip the leaves from the rosemary sprigs and scatter them over the dough.

13- Press them gently into the surface.

14- Sprinkle coarse sea salt evenly over the dough.

15- Bake the focaccia in the preheated oven for about 20-25 minutes, or until it is golden brown and sounds hollow when tapped on the bottom.

16- Once baked, remove the rosemary focaccia from the oven and let it cool slightly on a wire rack.

17- Slice and serve the onion-free rosemary focaccia as a fragrant and savory bread. Enjoy it on its own, with olive oil for dipping, or alongside soups, salads, and main dishes.

Note: This onion-free rosemary focaccia features a light and airy texture with the aromatic essence of rosemary. The simple yet flavorful topping creates a delicious and versatile bread perfect for sharing with family and friends. Customize the recipe by adjusting the amount of rosemary and salt to your preference. Savor the delightful taste and aroma of this classic Italian bread.

6.2. Cheddar and Chive Biscuits (Onion-Free)

Yield: 10-12 biscuits

Ingredients:

- 2 cups all-purpose flour
- 2 teaspoons baking powder
- 1/2 teaspoon baking soda
- 1/2 teaspoon salt
- 1/2 cup unsalted butter, cold and cubed
- 1 cup sharp cheddar cheese, grated
- 2 tablespoons fresh chives, chopped
- 3/4 cup buttermilk

Instructions:

1- Preheat the oven to 425°F (220°C) and line a baking sheet with parchment paper.

2- In a large mixing bowl, whisk together the flour, baking powder, baking soda, and salt.

3- Add the cold and cubed butter to the dry ingredients. Use a pastry cutter or your fingers to work the butter into the flour until the mixture resembles coarse crumbs.

4- Stir in the grated cheddar cheese and chopped fresh chives until they are evenly distributed throughout the dough.

5- Make a well in the center of the mixture and pour in the buttermilk.

6- Gently mix the dough with a fork or spatula until it comes together. Do not overmix; the dough should be slightly shaggy.

7- Turn the dough out onto a floured surface and pat it into a rectangle that's about 1-inch thick.

8- Use a round biscuit cutter to cut out biscuits from the dough. Press straight down without twisting to ensure the biscuits rise evenly.

9- Place the biscuits on the prepared baking sheet, leaving a little space between each one.

10- Gather any scraps of dough, pat them together, and cut out more biscuits.

11- Bake the cheddar and chive biscuits in the preheated oven for about 12-15 minutes, or until they are golden brown and cooked through.

12- Once baked, remove the biscuits from the oven and let them cool slightly on a wire rack.

13- Serve the onion-free cheddar and chive biscuits warm as a delightful and savory side. Enjoy them with butter, jam, or as a complement to soups, stews, or salads.

Note: These onion-free cheddar and chive biscuits offer a wonderful combination of sharp cheddar cheese and aromatic chives. The flaky and tender texture of the biscuits makes them a perfect accompaniment to a variety of meals. Customize the recipe by adjusting the amount of cheese and chives to your liking. Indulge in the comforting and flavorful taste of these classic homemade biscuits.

6.3. Herbed Dinner Rolls (Onion-Free)

Yield: Approximately 12-15 rolls

Ingredients:

For the Dough:

- 3 1/2 cups all-purpose flour
- 2 1/4 teaspoons active dry yeast
- 1 cup warm milk (about 110°F or 45°C)
- 1/4 cup unsalted butter, melted
- 2 tablespoons granulated sugar
- 1 teaspoon salt

For the Herbed Butter:

- 1/4 cup unsalted butter, softened
- 1 tablespoon fresh parsley, finely chopped
- 1 tablespoon fresh thyme leaves, chopped
- 1 tablespoon fresh rosemary, finely chopped
- Salt, to taste

Instructions:

For the Dough:

1- In a bowl, combine the warm milk and sugar. Sprinkle the active dry yeast over the milk mixture. Let it sit for about 5-10 minutes, or until the yeast becomes frothy.
2- In a large mixing bowl, combine the flour and salt.
3- Pour the yeast mixture and melted butter into the flour mixture. Stir until a dough forms.
4- Turn the dough out onto a floured surface and knead it for about 5-7 minutes, or until it becomes smooth and elastic.
5- Place the dough in a lightly oiled bowl, cover it with a damp cloth, and let it rise in a warm place for about 1 hour, or until it has doubled in size.

For the Herbed Butter:

1- In a small bowl, combine the softened butter, chopped parsley, chopped thyme, chopped rosemary, and a pinch of salt. Mix well to combine.

Assembly:

1- Preheat the oven to 375°F (190°C) and grease a baking pan or line it with parchment paper.
2- Punch down the risen dough and turn it out onto a floured surface.

3- Roll out the dough into a rectangle about 1/2-inch thick.

4- Spread the herbed butter evenly over the surface of the dough.

5- Starting from one edge, roll the dough tightly into a log.

6- Use a sharp knife or a bench scraper to cut the log into equal-sized rolls.

7- Place the rolls in the prepared baking pan, leaving a little space between each one.

8- Cover the pan with a damp cloth and let the rolls rise for about 30 minutes, or until they have puffed up.

9- Bake the herbed dinner rolls in the preheated oven for about 15-20 minutes, or until they are golden brown and cooked through.

10- Once baked, remove the rolls from the oven and let them cool slightly on a wire rack.

11- Serve the onion-free herbed dinner rolls warm as a flavorful and aromatic accompaniment to your meal.

Note: These onion-free herbed dinner rolls are enriched with a delightful blend of fresh herbs and butter. The soft and fluffy texture of the rolls makes them a wonderful addition to any dinner table. Customize the recipe by using your favorite herbs and adjusting the amount of herbed butter. Enjoy the comforting and fragrant taste of these homemade rolls that pair perfectly with soups, stews, roasts, and more.

6.4. Zucchini and Parmesan Muffins (Onion-Free)

Yield: Approximately 12 muffins

Ingredients:

- 1 1/2 cups all-purpose flour
- 1/2 cup grated Parmesan cheese
- 2 teaspoons baking powder
- 1/2 teaspoon baking soda
- 1/2 teaspoon salt
- 1/4 teaspoon freshly ground black pepper
- 1/2 teaspoon dried oregano
- 1/2 teaspoon dried thyme
- 1/2 cup milk
- 1/2 cup plain yogurt
- 1/4 cup unsalted butter, melted and cooled
- 1 large egg

- 1 1/2 cups grated zucchini, excess moisture squeezed out
- 2 tablespoons fresh parsley, finely chopped

Instructions:

1- Preheat the oven to 375°F (190°C) and line a muffin tin with paper liners or grease the cups.

2- In a large mixing bowl, whisk together the flour, grated Parmesan cheese, baking powder, baking soda, salt, freshly ground black pepper, dried oregano, and dried thyme.

3- In a separate bowl, whisk together the milk, plain yogurt, melted butter, and egg until well combined.

4- Pour the wet ingredients into the dry ingredients and gently fold until just combined. Do not overmix; a few lumps are okay.

5- Gently fold in the grated zucchini and chopped fresh parsley until evenly distributed throughout the batter.

6- Using a spoon or a scoop, divide the batter evenly among the muffin cups, filling each about two-thirds full.

7- Bake the zucchini and Parmesan muffins in the preheated oven for about 18-22 minutes, or until a toothpick inserted into the center of a muffin comes out clean.

8- Once baked, remove the muffins from the oven and let them cool in the muffin tin for a few minutes before transferring them to a wire rack to cool completely.

9- Serve the onion-free zucchini and Parmesan muffins as a savory and wholesome snack, breakfast, or side dish.

Note: These onion-free zucchini and Parmesan muffins offer a delightful combination of flavors and textures. The addition of grated zucchini provides moisture and nutrition to the muffins, while the Parmesan cheese adds a savory kick. Customize the recipe by adding other herbs or spices to your taste. Enjoy these delicious muffins as a tasty and satisfying treat that's perfect for any time of the day.

6.5. Chocolate Chip Banana Bread (Onion-Free)

Yield: 1 loaf

Ingredients:

- 2 to 3 ripe bananas, mashed (about 1 cup)
- 1/2 cup unsalted butter, melted

- 3/4 cup granulated sugar
- 2 large eggs
- 1 teaspoon vanilla extract
- 1 3/4 cups all-purpose flour
- 1 teaspoon baking soda
- 1/2 teaspoon salt
- 1/2 cup chocolate chips (semi-sweet or dark)

Instructions:

1- Preheat the oven to 350°F (175°C) and grease a 9x5-inch loaf pan or line it with parchment paper.

2- In a large mixing bowl, whisk together the melted butter and granulated sugar until well combined.

3- Add the mashed bananas, eggs, and vanilla extract to the bowl. Mix until the wet ingredients are thoroughly combined.

4- In a separate bowl, whisk together the all-purpose flour, baking soda, and salt.

5- Gradually add the dry ingredients to the wet ingredients, stirring until just combined. Do not overmix; a few lumps are okay.

6- Gently fold in the chocolate chips.

7- Pour the batter into the prepared loaf pan, spreading it evenly.

8- Bake the chocolate chip banana bread in the preheated oven for about 55-65 minutes, or until a toothpick inserted into the center comes out clean or with a few moist crumbs.

9- Once baked, remove the banana bread from the oven and let it cool in the pan for about 10 minutes before transferring it to a wire rack to cool completely.

Once completely cooled, slice the chocolate chip banana bread and serve.

Note: This chocolate chip banana bread is a moist and flavorful treat that combines the sweetness of ripe bananas with the richness of chocolate chips. The absence of onions ensures a pure and delightful taste. Customize the recipe by adding nuts, dried fruits, or other mix-ins if desired. Enjoy this classic and comforting baked good as a delightful snack, breakfast, or dessert.

7.1. Mixed Berry Crisp (Onion-Free)

Yield: 6-8 servings

Ingredients:

For the Berry Filling:

- 4 cups mixed berries (such as blueberries, raspberries, strawberries, and blackberries), fresh or frozen
- 1/4 cup granulated sugar
- 2 tablespoons cornstarch
- 1 tablespoon lemon juice
- 1 teaspoon vanilla extract

For the Crisp Topping:

- 1 cup old-fashioned rolled oats
- 1/2 cup all-purpose flour
- 1/2 cup packed brown sugar
- 1/2 teaspoon ground cinnamon
- 1/4 teaspoon salt
- 1/2 cup unsalted butter, cold and cut into small cubes

Instructions:

1- Preheat the oven to 350°F (175°C). Grease a 9x9-inch baking dish or a similar-sized oven-safe dish.
2- In a large bowl, gently toss together the mixed berries, granulated sugar, cornstarch, lemon juice, and vanilla extract until the berries are coated. Let the mixture sit for a few minutes to allow the flavors to combine.
3- Pour the berry mixture into the prepared baking dish, spreading it evenly. In a separate bowl, combine the rolled oats, all-purpose flour, brown sugar, ground cinnamon, and salt.
4- Add the cold butter cubes to the oat mixture. Use your fingers or a pastry cutter to work the butter into the dry ingredients until the mixture resembles coarse crumbs.
5- Sprinkle the crisp topping evenly over the berry filling. Place the baking dish on a baking sheet to catch any potential drips.

6- Bake the mixed berry crisp in the preheated oven for about 30-35 minutes, or until the filling is bubbly and the topping is golden brown.
7- Once baked, remove the crisp from the oven and let it cool slightly before serving.
8- Serve the onion-free mixed berry crisp warm, either on its own or with a scoop of vanilla ice cream or a dollop of whipped cream.

Note: This onion-free mixed berry crisp is a delightful and comforting dessert that showcases the natural sweetness and vibrant colors of mixed berries. The buttery oat topping adds a satisfying crunch to each bite. Customize the recipe by using your favorite combination of berries. Enjoy this cozy and delicious dessert on its own or with your preferred accompaniments for a delightful treat.

7.2. Vanilla Custard (Onion-Free)

Yield: 4-6 servings

Ingredients:

- 2 cups whole milk
- 1/2 cup granulated sugar
- 4 large egg yolks
- 1/4 cup cornstarch
- 1 teaspoon vanilla extract
- Pinch of salt
- Whipped cream, fresh berries, or a sprinkle of cinnamon (optional, for serving)

Instructions:

1- In a saucepan, heat the whole milk over medium heat until it starts to steam. Do not let it boil.
2- In a separate bowl, whisk together the granulated sugar, egg yolks, and cornstarch until the mixture is smooth and slightly pale.
3- Gradually pour a small amount of the steaming milk into the egg yolk mixture while whisking continuously. This tempers the egg yolks and prevents them from curdling.
4- Gradually whisk the tempered egg yolk mixture back into the remaining steaming milk in the saucepan.

5- Cook the mixture over medium heat, stirring constantly with a wooden spoon or silicone spatula, until it thickens and coats the back of the spoon. This will take about 5-7 minutes.

6- Remove the saucepan from the heat and stir in the vanilla extract and a pinch of salt.

7- Strain the custard through a fine-mesh sieve into a clean bowl to remove any lumps or cooked egg bits.

8- Place a piece of plastic wrap directly on the surface of the custard to prevent a skin from forming.

9- Let the vanilla custard cool to room temperature, then refrigerate it for at least 2 hours or until chilled and set.

10- Once chilled, give the custard a gentle stir to make it smooth again.

11- Serve the onion-free vanilla custard in individual dessert bowls. You can enjoy it as is or with optional toppings such as whipped cream, fresh berries, or a sprinkle of cinnamon.

Note: This onion-free vanilla custard is a luscious and creamy dessert with the classic flavor of vanilla. It can be enjoyed on its own or used as a base for other desserts like fruit tarts, parfaits, or trifles. Customize the recipe by adding other flavorings or extracts if desired. Indulge in the silky texture and rich taste of this timeless dessert.

7.3. Apple Cinnamon Galette (Onion-Free)

Yield: 6-8 servings

Ingredients:

For the Pastry Dough:

- 1 1/4 cups all-purpose flour
- 1/4 teaspoon salt
- 1/2 cup unsalted butter, cold and cubed
- 3-4 tablespoons ice water

For the Apple Filling:

- 3-4 medium apples, peeled, cored, and thinly sliced
- 1/4 cup granulated sugar
- 1 teaspoon ground cinnamon
- 1 tablespoon lemon juice

- 1 tablespoon unsalted butter, melted (for brushing)

For Assembly and Garnish:

- 1 tablespoon granulated sugar (for sprinkling)
- 1 tablespoon apricot preserves or fruit jelly (for glaze)

Instructions:

For the Pastry Dough:

1- In a mixing bowl, whisk together the all-purpose flour and salt.
2- Add the cold and cubed butter to the flour mixture. Use a pastry cutter or your fingers to work the butter into the flour until the mixture resembles coarse crumbs.
3- Gradually add the ice water, one tablespoon at a time, and mix until the dough comes together. Be careful not to overmix.
4- Shape the dough into a disc, wrap it in plastic wrap, and refrigerate for at least 30 minutes.

For the Apple Filling:

1- In a bowl, toss the thinly sliced apples with granulated sugar, ground cinnamon, and lemon juice until the apples are coated.

Assembly and Baking:

1- Preheat the oven to 375°F (190°C) and line a baking sheet with parchment paper.
2- On a floured surface, roll out the chilled pastry dough into a rough circle about 12 inches in diameter.
3- Carefully transfer the rolled-out dough onto the prepared baking sheet.
4- Arrange the apple slices in the center of the dough, leaving a border of about 2 inches all around.
5- Fold the edges of the dough over the apple filling, pleating as you go, to create a rustic galette shape.
6- Brush the edges of the dough with melted butter and sprinkle granulated sugar over the exposed apple slices.
7- Bake the apple cinnamon galette in the preheated oven for about 30-35 minutes, or until the crust is golden brown and the apples are tender.

8- Once baked, remove the galette from the oven and let it cool slightly on the baking sheet.

9- In a small saucepan, heat the apricot preserves or fruit jelly over low heat until melted. Brush the melted preserves over the apple slices for a glossy finish.

10- Serve the onion-free apple cinnamon galette warm or at room temperature. It can be enjoyed on its own or with a scoop of vanilla ice cream or a dollop of whipped cream.

Note: This onion-free apple cinnamon galette is a delightful dessert that showcases the comforting flavors of apples and cinnamon in a rustic and elegant presentation. The flaky pastry crust and tender apple filling create a perfect balance of textures. Customize the recipe by adding other spices or nuts if desired. Enjoy this simple and flavorful treat that captures the essence of fall and comfort.

7.4. Chocolate Avocado Mousse (Onion-Free)

Yield: 4-6 servings

Ingredients:

- 2 ripe avocados, peeled and pitted
- 1/4 cup unsweetened cocoa powder
- 1/4 cup honey or maple syrup
- 1 teaspoon vanilla extract
- 1/4 cup milk (dairy or non-dairy)
- Pinch of salt
- Optional toppings: whipped cream, shaved chocolate, berries, chopped nuts

Instructions:

1- In a food processor or blender, combine the ripe avocados, unsweetened cocoa powder, honey or maple syrup, vanilla extract, milk, and a pinch of salt.

2- Blend the ingredients until smooth and creamy, scraping down the sides of the bowl as needed.

3- Taste the chocolate avocado mixture and adjust the sweetness if desired by adding more honey or maple syrup.

4- Once the mixture is smooth and well combined, divide it into serving cups or glasses.

5- Refrigerate the chocolate avocado mousse for at least 1-2 hours to allow it to chill and set.
6- Before serving, you can top the mousse with optional toppings such as whipped cream, shaved chocolate, berries, or chopped nuts.
7- Serve the onion-free chocolate avocado mousse as a rich and indulgent dessert. Enjoy its velvety texture and chocolatey flavor without the need for onions.

Note: This onion-free chocolate avocado mousse is a healthier alternative to traditional mousse recipes, thanks to the creamy goodness of avocados. The natural sweetness from honey or maple syrup complements the rich cocoa flavor, creating a decadent treat. Customize the recipe by adjusting the sweetness and toppings to your preference. Delight in the guilt-free pleasure of this satisfying dessert that's both delicious and nutritious.

7.5. Coconut Rice Pudding (Onion-Free)

Yield: 4-6 servings

Ingredients:

- 1 cup jasmine or basmati rice
- 1 can (14 oz) coconut milk (full-fat)
- 2 cups milk (dairy or non-dairy)
- 1/2 cup granulated sugar
- 1/2 teaspoon vanilla extract
- 1/4 teaspoon salt
- 1/2 cup sweetened shredded coconut
- Ground cinnamon or nutmeg, for garnish (optional)
- Toasted coconut flakes, for garnish (optional)

Instructions:

1- Rinse the rice under cold water until the water runs clear. This helps remove excess starch.
2- In a medium saucepan, combine the rinsed rice, coconut milk, milk, and granulated sugar.
3- Place the saucepan over medium heat and bring the mixture to a gentle simmer. Stir occasionally to prevent sticking.

4- Reduce the heat to low and let the rice simmer, partially covered, for about 30-40 minutes, or until the rice is cooked and the mixture has thickened. Stir occasionally to prevent scorching.

5- Once the rice is cooked and the mixture is thickened, remove the saucepan from the heat.

6- Stir in the vanilla extract, salt, and sweetened shredded coconut.

7- Let the coconut rice pudding cool slightly before serving.

8- Serve the onion-free coconut rice pudding warm or chilled in individual dessert bowls.

9- If desired, garnish each serving with a sprinkle of ground cinnamon or nutmeg, as well as toasted coconut flakes for added flavor and texture.

Note: This onion-free coconut rice pudding is a creamy and comforting dessert that features the tropical flavors of coconut. The sweetened shredded coconut adds a delightful chewiness to each spoonful. Customize the recipe by adjusting the sweetness and coconut content to your preference. Enjoy this luscious and aromatic dessert that's perfect for satisfying your sweet cravings.

Conclusion:

Thank you for embarking on this flavorful journey of onion-free cooking with us. We hope these recipes have inspired you to create delicious meals without compromising on taste. Remember, the joy of cooking lies in experimentation and creativity. Feel free to modify and customize these recipes to suit your preferences and dietary needs. Happy cooking!

Printed in Great Britain
by Amazon